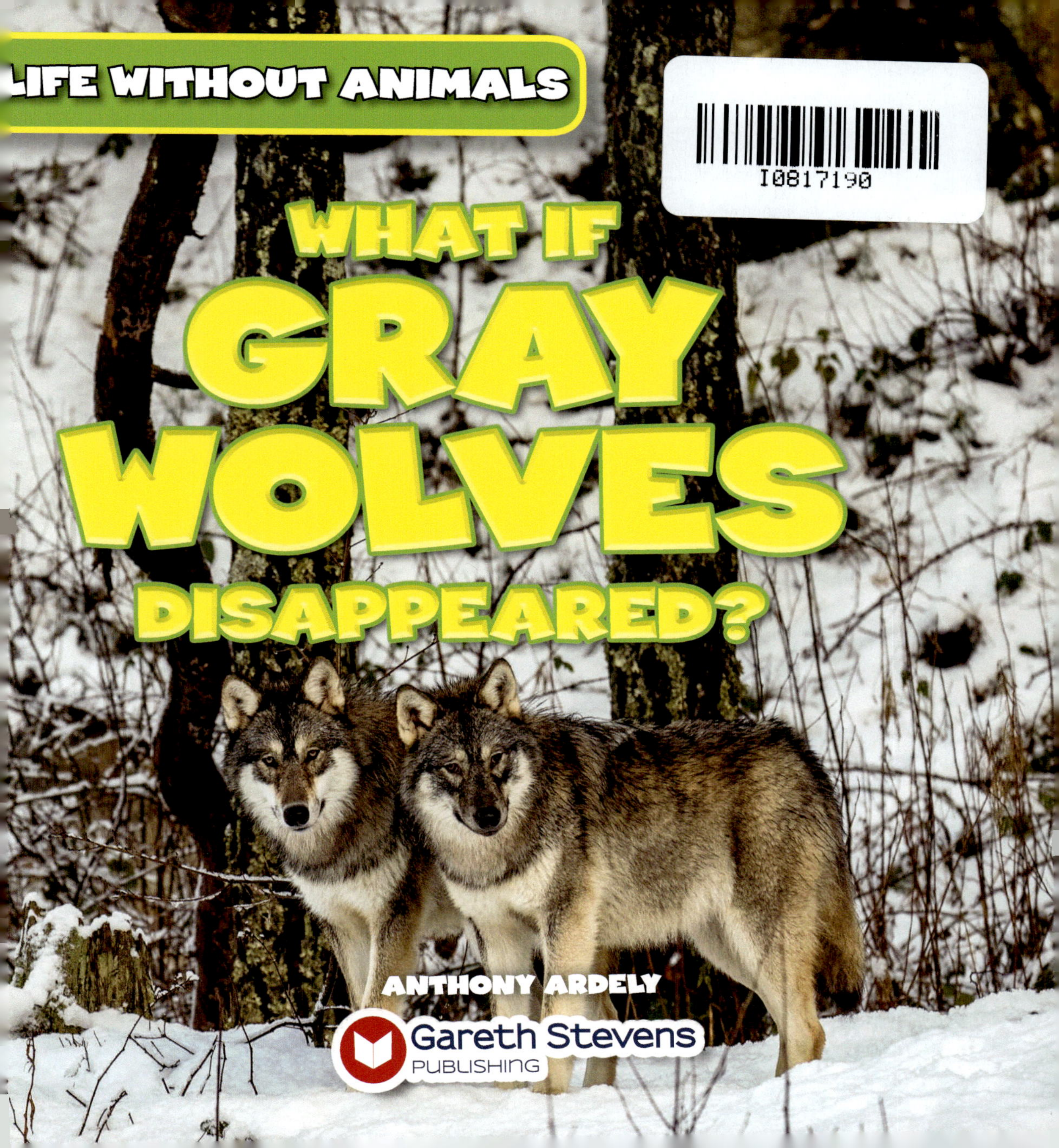
LIFE WITHOUT ANIMALS
I0817190
WHAT IF
GRAY
WOLVES
DISAPPEARED?
ANTHONY ARDELY
Gareth Stevens
PUBLISHING

Please visit our website, www.garethstevens.com. For a free color catalog of all our high-quality books, call toll free 1-800-542-2595 or fax 1-877-542-2596.

Library of Congress Cataloging-in-Publication Data

Names: Ardely, Anthony, author.
Title: What if gray wolves disappeared? / Anthony Ardely.
Description: New York : Gareth Stevens Publishing, [2023] | Series: Life without animals | Includes index.
Identifiers: LCCN 2021045429 | ISBN 9781538276327 (set) | ISBN 9781538276334 (library binding) | ISBN 9781538276310 (paperback) | ISBN 9781538276341 (ebook)
Subjects: LCSH: Gray wolf–Juvenile literature. | Gray wolf–Behavior–Juvenile literature. | Gray wolf–Conservation–Juvenile literature.
Classification: LCC QL737.C22 A73 2023 | DDC 599.773–dc23
LC record available at https://lccn.loc.gov/2021045429

Published in 2023 by
Gareth Stevens Publishing
111 East 14th Street, Suite 349
New York, NY 10003

Designer: Rachel Rising
Editor: Kate Mikoley

Photo credits: Cover, p.1 By Lillian Tveit/Shutterstock.com; pp. 3, 4, 6, 8, 10, 12, 14, 16, 18, 20,22-24 Igor Kyrlytsya/Shutterstock.com; p. 5 Jim Cumming/Shutterstock.com; p. 7 Holly Kuchera/Shutterstock.com; p. 9 Michal Ninger/Shutterstock.com; p. 11 AB Photographie/Shutterstock.com; p. 13 Warren Metcalf/Shutterstock.com; p. 15 topseller/Shutterstock.com; p. 17 Sergey Uryadnikov/Shutterstock.com; p. 19 Danita Delimont/Shutterstock.com; p. 21 Tomas Hejlek/Shutterstock.com.

Printed in the United States of America

CPSIA compliance information: Batch #CSGS23: For further information contact Gareth Stevens, New York, New York at 1-800-542-2595.

CONTENTS

Boldface words appear in the glossary.

Get to Know Gray Wolves

Gray wolves are the largest animals in the dog family. They live in groups called packs. These wolves are known for being smart and skilled at hunting. Together, a pack can hunt and kill animals much larger than the wolves themselves.

Gray wolves are sometimes called timber wolves. They live in parts of North America, Europe, and Asia. As their name suggests, gray wolves commonly have gray fur. However, their fur can also be brown, black, white, or red.

Keystone Species

Gray wolves may be a **threat** to the animals they hunt, but they also help keep **ecosystems** healthy. In fact, gray wolves are known as a keystone **species**. This is a species other animals and plants **depend** on.

If a keystone species were to disappear, the ecosystem they left would face big changes. In some cases, it could even go away altogether. If gray wolves disappeared, many other species would be in danger.

On the Hunt

Gray wolves are the top predators in their ecosystems. They commonly hunt large animals such as elk, bison, moose, and deer. Without wolves, the **populations** of these animals could become too large.

BISON

The animals that gray wolves hunt are important too, but ecosystems are all about **balance**. Gray wolves' **prey** are often animals that eat **vegetation**. If the populations of these animals grew too large, the plants they eat could go away, harming important **habitats**.

Feeding Other Animals

Other animals sometimes get their meals from animals gray wolves kill. Scavengers are animals that eat the remains of dead animals. Certain birds, foxes, coyotes, and bears are just some animals that may get their food from gray wolf kills.

Gone and Brought Back

Sometimes, gray wolves attack and kill farm animals. For this reason, people have killed them throughout history. In the United States, gray wolves were nearly all killed off by 1950. However, groups worked to bring them back. In the late 20th century, they were **reintroduced** in many areas.

Protecting Gray Wolves

In places where gray wolves nearly disappeared, ecosystems became unbalanced. Some animal populations grew too large, while some plant species nearly disappeared. Today, gray wolves are protected in some areas by government programs.

GLOSSARY

balance: a state in which different things happen in equal or proper amounts

depend: to need

ecosystem: all the living things in an area

habitat: the natural place where an animal or plant lives

population: the number of animals of the same kind that live in a place

prey: an animal that is hunted by other animals for food

reintroduce: to return an animal or plant population back to the area where it used to live

species: a group of plants or animals that are all of the same kind

threat: something likely to cause harm

vegetation: trees, bushes, and other plants

FOR MORE INFORMATION

BOOKS

Borgert-Spaniol, Megan. *Gray Wolves: Yellowstone's Hunters.* Minneapolis, MN: Abdo Publishing, 2020.

Rustad, Martha E. H. *A Pack of Wolves.* North Mankato, MN: Pebble, 2020.

Statts, Leo. *Wolves.* Minneapolis, MN: Abdo Zoom, 2020.

WEBSITES

Gray Wolf
kids.nationalgeographic.com/animals/mammals/facts/gray-wolf
Watch a short video and read more fascinating facts about these cool creatures.

Gray Wolf
www.biokids.umich.edu/critters/Canis_lupus/
Learn more about gray wolves on this website from the University of Michigan.

INDEX